FrogFur

CW00966621

Once upon a time a few mud hills away. There was a little frog called FrogFur from Pondlake.

FrogFur was blue with a chubby build just under 1ft tall. Up above his tree house outside his window he could see the gates of Chestnut City and down below warm deep rivers. The great giant Lily-pads, floating river boats and smoked oak tree huts peeping through the trees. Dangling ropes, stinging nettle bushes, stick ladders, pine cabins on wheels like wooden shed caravans plodding through muddy roads. The surrounding rivers ripping with daffodils and buttercups, tiny pots of colour sweeping through reservoirs under the hills. A wonderfully busy place where FrogFur suddenly found himself on an adventure.

A few frogs leaps away, FrogFur was sitting outside a small café that sold baked beans on toast and lemon tea. The river gates opened each day at sunrise and he could watch the boats pull in from the city. He had no idea that later that day things were about to change.

Princess Chip, Princess of Chestnut City had reigned surrounding ponds and villages after her late father King Roy. Many years ago a young farmer set traps in the reservoir and made a terrible mistake may he had made. A trap had caught something in the forest and when the swim guards searched? They found his crown and cloak but not King Roy.

Princess Chip, saddened by the disappearance of her father, lived with her sisters in the extraordinary palace. The entire palace dances in acres of vineyards growing the sweetest red grapes made for wine.

Chip enjoyed making wine and gathered crates in the garden with her guards for festivals and markets. Something new. King Roy was never so kind or endearing and FrogFur after his parents were killed finessed in the cultural flamboyance of the pond, hidden in rivers funky spots like the cafe le dandy.

FrogFur's breakfast was plated as he said hello to Bugger and Barbican sailing in from the Locks. His newspaper now spread to page four of a huge mural of former water sports champions Freddy Frogger and Famillion Foxworth. He glances up at the city horizon now covered in morning fog from a distance.

Jade had curly brown hair and whiskers that twitched when she lied. She was travelling around outside the palace. She was fond of Pondlake and the characters her father told when she was a small squirrel trying to make sense of the world. Rebecca was on a date despite numerous requests not to. She was always disobedient since her father went missing. She held no pity for peasants and authority.

Even though they were different in age, all three sisters were never too busy for 'The Legends Of The Lakes'. The race which happens once every white moon. A sporting triumph with water racing and hikes, television coverage and camping. Princess Chip was excited. It was a chance for her to relax and spend all day cheering and eating custard ant cakes with pumpkin pie.

PondLake

A wet splodge of mud hits a tree. Welp. FrogFur dashes pass with a handful of conkers. Three shifty foxes and a skinny Foxer follow him close with quick legs.
As the next mud pie whispers pass his ear, he ducks and swerves running fast up a muddy hill. Splish, Splash. Splosh. His webbed feet clenched in the mud.

Foxer draws his last mud pie, mud and tree bark mixed with water in a biscuit tin funneled into an old sock and launches it in the air. It splatters another tree. FrogFur slides down another muddy hill towards the pond. Splat! mud splashing everywhere. DOuble rolled into a moving mud river which led through to PondLake where the foxes were forbidden to go.

They stood by the willow tree and buttercup vines howling disturbing slurs.

'Maybe next time fox face.' FrogFur shouts stuffing conkers and coins into his pockets.

The market was in Mudhill Village where Foxer and his cousins lived. Foxer and FrogFur were cold blooded enemies but nobody knew why. I will describe more about the place or actually explain how I know about this story.

A few canal streams later at home in his tree house FrogFur fills his kettle pot to make a gorgeous cup of chestnut coffee. The tree lights lit up as the sun sank down below the hills. The garden lanterns sat gently as the canal boats slowly crept home for the night.

FrogFur was chubby with shiny teal skin and freckles just under 1ft tall. His casual attire was that of woodland fashion. He fried a few conkers to make them crispy just as the kettle finished whistling.

'A lovely cup of chestnut coffee.' he smiles, switching on the telly.

His flatmate Buxley 'a flying pig' worked in a boat house and wasn't yet home. FrogFur left the tree house window open and got into his hammock. The silent crackles from the pond eased to silence all but the crickets could be heard humming in the distance.

The next day was sports registration. The Legends of the Lakes. Everyone gathered by Leap lane.

The fish swam in luminous wetsuits, the eels snorkelling through the lower streams and the reservoirs making sure the drains were functioning. The cold water splashing up on to the banks at the dawn of day smelling like chlorine flowers dripping after a rainstorm, spitefully fresh.

The air balloons and pop up shops planted in open streams playing music. The canal boats paddled past whilst others walked admiring the architectural echalance of Pond Lake. Each river lit up with hanging light jars and neighbours gardens also encouraged dandy lights and mud baths in the front gardens.

FrogFur stood at the back of the queue with his arm bands on. His flying guardian Buxley flew above his head in his flower waistcoat. The frog registration table was a pop up stall with a few leaves shading the old toads on red and white beach chairs. The larger toad had a big purple pimple just above his green lips, scribbling notes on his paper.

'So what are you going to try today? Walk and splash or tumble and drown?'

'Please Buxley, I don't need your fucking sarcasm today. I need you to help keep that Foxer out of my way. I have it under control.'

He squeezed his arm bands on tight and checked his snorkel tube. The crowd cheered in the background with excitement. FrogFur, despite his fear of heights, signed up with Buxley. He noticed the hysterical chaos the foxes and squirrels were causing on the opposite side. The foxes were playing drill music and hollering loud suggestive words across the river to the squirrels.

The squirrels known for fashion and celebrity simply ignored and carried on registration.

Sid the snowboarding Squirrel from Australia surfed in on a new crowded boat full of rabbits dressed in celine bathing suits with clean hair and make up. He was very popular and talented. Most magazines would pay a thousand gold crowns just to see him. He was sports squirrel of the year and filthy rich.

FrogFur signed the sports sheet and walked over to the river to wet his lips. His pulsing silk skin reflected in the water. Refreshing.

The short toad comes over and shoves the number seven jersey in Buxley's backpack with a few tools and a notepad with some pens.

FrogFur helped move their bags. He looked suave and savvy, a true allegiant of leap frog dynasty. He read the forms aloud as Buxley called for a canal boat to take them upstream.

"The next few days of gruelling challenges will be in muddy water and windy winds. This new moon, Legend of the Lakes is set to be a wet display of boating , hiking and flying. This Pond is known for its beautiful serene ponds and tranquil rivers. Any cheating will be disqualified. The first to complete all challenges will win.

He looked around, nobody looked bothered, maybe the hot sun and atmosphere helped ease the evil that lay nesting in the races ahead.

Lets not forget that whoever won would be appointed a noble guardian of the pond, honoured with a gold championship winners cup, a thousand acres of sweet honeysuckle bushes, 3 boats, and the secret ingredient to breed wishing worms. Wishing worms were magical, some say a myth but nevertheless they worked wonders for many kings and queens of the pond for many years.

Sir Tod, a tall aristocratic grasshopper, made notes as the canal locks began to fill. He received a travel note for a cab which he sent out straight away. His slinky lean face with his slender popping eyes sort to be a smooth interlude to gate security at the docks, barracks and locks.

Sir Tod had married a princess butterfly called Matilda. She had four kids until she ran off with some new cricket called Carl. She took the boys but left her grandchild Spec. Princess Spec they called her. She was a cute Frog. Princess purple with freckles. Her best friend Pheobe lived with them too. Sir Tod took care of the girls whilst his estranged wife moved in with Carl and pretty much never wrote.

The Locks.

Most boats carried food, drink, wood and other odd things. It was a Grasshopper business. A very attentive job. Not much interaction, a lot of searching and paperwork. It was fun though. The Locks was a clanky place with lots of metal pipes laying around. Bolts and screws in paint pots and Sir Tod's home under the bridge was like a huge barrel that got left behind by a giant.

The canal cab turns up to pick up Buxley and FrogFur with their bags.

'You would think Tod would have some tips for us, he is always cattling at some old boats for tools? He's probably so busy at the locks today. Look at this place, it is overcrowded.'

'His to old to even notice we are in the race let alone help'

'Hahahahahahhahah' laughs FrogFur.

The cab driver was a small brown mouse with gold grills. He wasn't amused at the conversation but kindly asked for the address.

'If you don't keep quiet you will be wingless soon enough. Do you remember no legs lee? He said some sort of challenge will test our ability to synchronise and you can't swim?

'Yes I remember he was crazy. Jumping from an air balloon without a parachute does usually end much worse. Now think of him chasing you and you will win that first challenge'

'A cricket? with no legs? chasing me? He replies and laughs again.

This time the mouse gets an attitude and shouts to the back of the cab.

'Where am I going?'

'Oh sorry, 15 Leap River near the willow trees' replied Buxley

The cab floats down past the parking lot into the main river to take them home. The streams had been plodded with underwater lights. All the news stations were arriving. Solar panels were being drilled into the wooden cabins to power the generators. The Pond was transforming.
Wireless microphones, stage lights, lots of kerfuffle around the restaurants. Cameras twirling trying to capture everything as this magical place became even more magical. A news reporter stood in front of her camera in her dress dripping across the floor. Action.

'We are here in a wondrous pond. Pond Lake. Why? It is a celebration. Undeniably the most talked about sporting event. Some of us will be attending for the first time. We are here to livestream the next few days the Legends Of The Lakes sponsored by Chestnut Commercial and Tech Blast.

I will be taking a tour around and reporting backstage news of what's going on. I am yanka khans and this is GBC NEWS'

Her draping river dress slid across the grass sparkling as the baby moths and butterflies helped lift from underneath making her appear to glide across the water.

Her dress was Indian gold with rose red diamonds reflecting in the water like a crystal blood diamond. Her diamond necklace was given to her by her father King Sham of Tiger Town in India. Her news channel had paid for her hotel in mudhill village and the restaurant opposite served the best grub.

Yanker was a slender curvy frog with slit eyes stretching along her cupcake skin. Her podcast which had over five million subscribers was very popular and she had many fans.

She started presenting on a comedy show 'ka Badsshah - Hasega India' and somehow was booked for Legend Of The Lakes a few months back. Her pet bird was a tropical parrot and was ever so handy when she was live reporting.

The rest of the news stations started to squabble around, anxiously waiting to see if they could get through the locks, this was a sold out event. Princess Spec and her fairly large voice was in charge of checking passes and directing traffic. She checked every single boat and barge, all two hundred of them that day. Phoebe just walked around looking busy but not doing much work. Tod ordered a scrumptious take-away from Bug Kebabs as the night drew to a close.

'Right, that's the last boat Spec' said Tod.

They pulled the rain cover over the lock and went inside the barrel for supper.

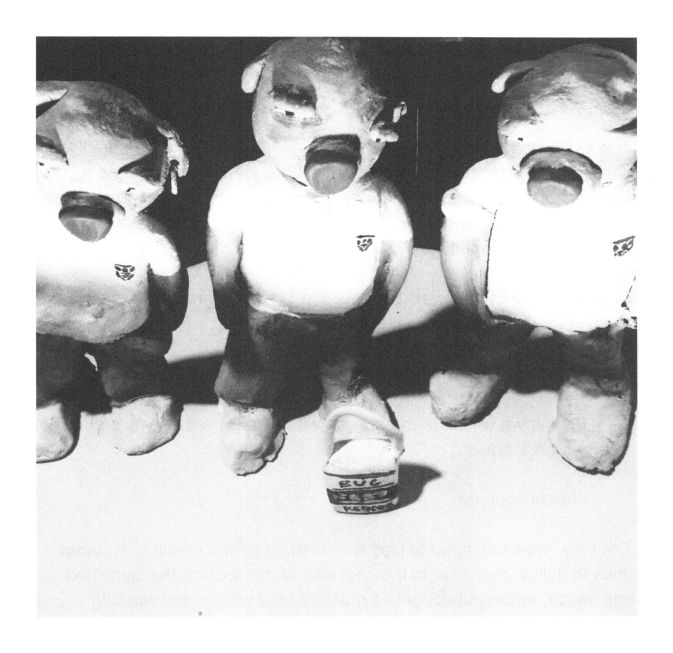

Bug Kebabs

A trendy kebab house restaurant and take-away in Pondlake. A traditional family business. Fresh mouth watering bug kebabs using authentic turkish recipes. The most advanced cooking methods with ingredients grown in the harvesting fields of Mudhill village. The taste is well known for its juicy succulent bugs with ice cold Milk-Flie-Shakes.

Crispy caterpillar shells with grass guacamole. Mustard mud worms. The barbeque bug burger with grilled slugs and toasted buttercups. It was delicious food.

The smell of the cold river with smoky grilled grub had the nostril hairs dancing. FrogFur and his good friend Alber were hoping to get a good table. The rain had started sprinkling on the walk up and Buxley had gone to work on the boat at the boathouse. The boat that was going to win the race he hoped.

FrogFur stood by the crab tank outside scrolling through the menu, his wet fingers dabbling across his chin.

'What can I get you and this beautiful fish tonight?'

'I think we will taste the special with extra grilled worms and a seat by the window.'

'Yes of course.'

The band was setting up to play a few songs for the evening. Hussain goes to deliver the order to the chef who starts cooking the chips and egg sauce, sweet potato, grilled mustard mud worms and two bug burgers.

Alber was extremely happy to have a window seat, she was a fascinating fish and loved the rain.

Alber and FrogFur met when he was a small tadpole. She sipped her water which meant she was about to start a difficult conversation. They were best friends.

'So.....The infamous FrogFur is about to be an olympian of the lakes. This I have to see.'

'If the river is kind I will win what is mine.' he reveals.

'I would like to be involved. Any ideas of what tent you'll be using?' Alber replies hysterically.

'Buxley has everything sorted but thanks.'

'Buxley is a control freak. He needs to let you have fun.'

'He will warm to the idea soon enough. We are just happy to be a team to be honest. Apart from you nobody else knows these rivers like us'

Alber was bottle green with blushing pooched lips. Her crop top and glasses complemented her stylish geek fashion. She was a very strong swimmer. She knew FrogFur from Pond School. As the plates were laid on the table, Albers phone rang. It was chat show host Grey-ham Norton the swedish pig.

'Grey, Thanks for calling me back, how are you? Yes, fabulous. It looks fabulous. We are incredibly excited to be doing this for you. I promise you the designs are fantastic! Light streams strobing around! Flamboyancy. Sounds great! Dancing Russian rabbits ...? we can make that happen. Yes. Okay. Bye Grey.'

Alber's gills were flapping and FrogFur was eager to hear the news. Grey-ham had approved her designs and wanted to add dancing Russian rabbits in the opening scene of his show. The late night set in the treehouse she had just finished designing. She ordered several antinis from the bar.

Chives

Chives was a restored tree house basement, decked out with wooden interior, oil stone tables with chunky grass hedge sofas, eastern lanterns dropping from the ceiling like curtains.
Alber and her friends sat sipping seaweed cocktails talking to the Russian Rabbits who just signed the contract for the opening show tomorrow.

The bouncers outside were two chunky foxes who didn't allow everyone and anyone in. One had several tattoos on his face, the other had red hair with a red beard like a rock n roll santa. The door list was extremely long and the wait was about an hour.

The club closed at 4am and the place was boiling with fancy celebrities and high spenders. The music played loud echoing down the river like a bumblebee stuck in a plastic bottle. She left FrogFur and Hussain at the restaurant hours before and enjoyed her night with the girls.

Training Day

The next few days Buxley took charge of the shopping trips. He incorporated a water and lemon diet into their daily meals at home. A rota was hung up by the fridge and the training weights had been delivered. All the biscuits and slug pies had been stored next door at Julie's house and the biscuit tin was hidden under the hammock in Buxleys room.

They trained a few hours a day. Lifting and chopping wood. Buxley was trying his best to get FrogFur to use the rowing machine at the boathouse to strengthen his legs. He wanted FrogFur to concentrate on his training and nothing else. He made FrogFur run up and down the hills at night and got him to learn how to use a slingshot with conkers.

FrogFur didn't enjoy the diet but was beginning to look like a real athlete so he kept training and drank the lemon water every morning, noon and night.

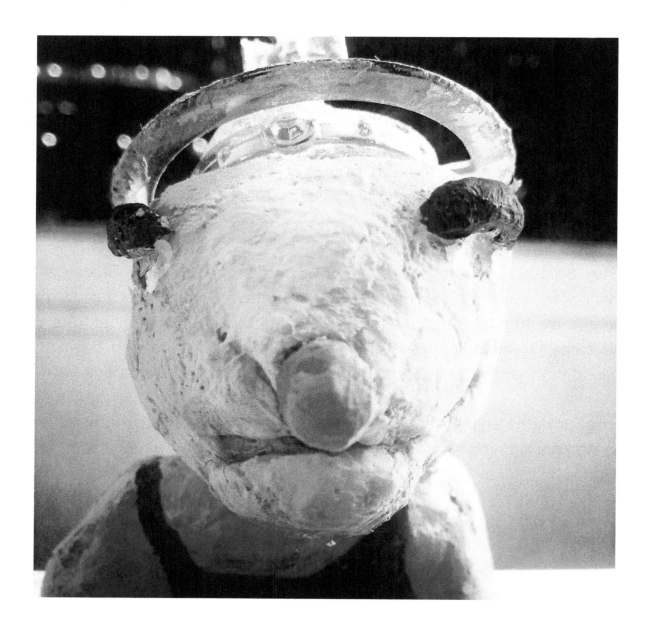

Barbican's Lodge

The sun was beginning to dance down below the clouds. Barbican and his wife were in their treehouse lodge. The smell of red mushrooms, warm milk, blowing through the chimney. Barbican had gathered the majority of ingredients the night before. Bae was scrolling through a cookery book in her handmade grass apron.

'The nutmeg and milk are boiling nicely dear. Do you have the magic ingredient?' says Barbican stirring the large pot on the fire hob.

'I guess we can add it in. It's the best of the last. Last of the best. Best something. I couldn't catch what he said. You know what FrogFur's like always in a hurry.' his wife mutters.

Barbican takes his glasses off his nose pausing with disappointment.

'So it's stolen?' he snaps. 'How can we present this offering to the princess with stolen ingredients?'

'I promised him you would not judge him for his efforts. This is not just for us. The entire village is excited to see him compete. Nobody has to know.'

She takes the hot tray of biscuits from the oven to cool ready for decoration.

'It is skullduggery. I don't want to get into trouble with Foxer. He was chosen as guardian of this village which is why we should tread lightly.'

'We cannot ignore things that need our attention.' replies Bae happily.

She heads to the balcony to gather fresh butter cups for the icing of the biscuits. Barbican had always had high hopes for FrogFur since he was a small tadpole playing in the tiny streams with Alber.

Bae opens the jar labelled "wishing worms" and pours the jar into the large iron pot. The pot glows a tropical rainbow colour and starts to boil. The kitchen was covered in hanging garlic, fuchsia brown velvet flowers and maps of places they had visited. At the front dining area was a large table with envelopes and other stationary equipment.

As Barbican was secretary to the patron of Chestnut City his work dominated the lodge. His painting of Chip, Able, Foxer and Studley hung above their fireplace in a sparkling gold cupid frame. The outside garden was decorated with her wonderful cherry trees and buttercup flowers. The balcony was set with running water sprinklers which wet the porch every night. Beautiful red mushroom baskets, honeysuckle bushes split along the path on both sides leading to what looked like an old church yard door.

The large tree next door belonged to the largest tree house according to the local swim guards. This tree housed over 2,000 red and grey squirrels. The mother was loud and large so she rarely left the top floor. You could hear her shout for her kids every morning. Some had never seen her before in the pond nor at the market. Her children ran in and out like field mice caught on fire and hardly kept the noise down. Since Barbican and Bae never had children they never complained and grew to enjoy living next to them.

Barbican gathered the bottles ready for delivery. He grabbed his walking stick and made his way outside. He took out his glasses and began to sort out the bottles in location order. Each bottle listed and made to measure.

The delivery for the grand deluxe suite in Chestnut City was wrapped in a velvet red cloth.

The post collection boat arrived. A small bug was at the door with a list. His name was Bugger. Bugger never spoke, only delivered and collected posts. He was small and had orphan feet. Everyday before noon he'd whizzed around the treehouses in his canal boat collecting and delivering mail. His elder cousin was a dressmaker called Bamear from Chestnut City.

Barbican was back indoors with a sigh of relief that he had finished his appointed job and sat down with his pondlake newspaper. They sat at the table to eat tea, worm porridge, ant eggs and the biscuits with the buttercup icing. A fashionable ferret breakfast, fit for a ferret.

FrogFur and his family had been the greatest jumpers in leapfrog history. Their trophies and pictures hung in the corridors at the local museum. FrogFur looked in the mirror and admired how huge and solid his body was. His arms were now of muscle and his legs seemed more jumpy than usual, he could jump the first three branches to the house without a sweat.

He sat by a small lily stream pondering his thoughts, overlooking the tree hubs covered in pink roses like colourful butterfly wings when they flutter at sea. The sweet warm milk martini dripped down his chin as buxley flew down to hand him his official legends of the lakes letter. He sat next to FrogFur with an airy look on his face.

'FrogFur don't fuck this up.'

A few hours later after training they went home. The tree house had been trashed. They called the local swim guard Able. He wrote a report about the damage. FrogFur was angry and went for a walk alone.

The next day Buxley was making a short snack, moth porridge and seaweed juice.

'So did you find out who did it?'.

'I went for a swim last night. I needed some time alone'.

'I cannot force you to train with me but we are in this together, you storming into the night like a vigilante, isn't proving teamwork?'.

'I understand. I will fix the Milk-O-Metre. We need it running before we push that boat into the water. Where is my toolbox? I need to finish making fly nets. I have to paint the paddles, and weld the night lights to the boat'.

'So us being detectives can wait?'

Buxley smiles and hands him his tool box. They drag the bubbled glass milk-o-metre machine from behind the berry bushes and throw the gel protector cover to the side. The milk-o-metre was high voltage boat engine equipment used to power the boat and pump milk bottles like an espresso machine. Frogfur got the screws and a lightbulb and worked on it until it switched on. A loud bang went off and the light bulb lit up. He let it run for a few minutes. It was working and he welded it to the inside of the boat propeller system and presto paisley the boat was doing 100mph in 7 secs.

So that night the news reporters were doing a backstage film on the competition. Pre dressed in a red swimsuit sat by her houseboat recording her voice over live.

'It is very quiet at the treehouses of Pondlake despite the visitors and Mudhill Village Foxes spending the night. So happy we are able to get a real inside look of what these magnificent tree hubs look like. In a mist of smoky fires and boiling teapots everyone seems calm so far. This is Pond Lake's last day of silence before this water race, legends of lakes begins. I am excited. Our favourites are all here. Our Canadian superstar Sid the snowboarding Squirrel, Foxer and Hugo from Mudhill Village. FrogFur a fan favourite, Breakfast Buxley the Flying Pig. All creatures great and small.
The challenge tomorrow is split into two. The first part is to hike through the fields using a machete, the deep thick mud clenching knee deep with mud bugs swarming like fish flies. Find their badge of legacy and complete the tunnel maze by nightfall. Let's hope everyone has packed their maps and equipment because once the race has started they will be unable to return home until a winner is crowned.'

Pre sat at the end of the boat with her glow stick kissing the river. She noticed FrogFur hoisting the milk-o-metre down from the high trees with rope showing his muscles. As she steers they both laugh. His pretty white teeth and lips catching Pre in a mirage of love.

Foxer and his cousins had set up camp on the opposite side of the river. They were very loud and leary and causing riot to the locals already. Clinking bottles and chuckling in a huddle, setting off rockets and fireworks. Foxer was popular and everyone had heard stories of dangerous things he had done. Once cutting a mice tail over a card game. He was also feared by many in the city.

'I know he had something to do with the house getting trashed.' he moans.

'Who?'

'Flaming Foxer' replies FrogFur

'Why would he?

'His been laughing all night and Carl the Cricket said they see him running through here last night after midnight'

Buxley pushed his legs through his tightly made swimsuit, sizing himself in the mirror to FrogFurs frustration. He tied the sail and turned on the night lamps, and flew to FrogFur who was paddle clenched in thought.

'Why do you let him wind you up?'. He replies.

'His scrawny face makes me want to go over there right now and thrash him in the face'

'fish blade, rope, stinging nettle cream, belt spikes for climbing, a new paddle, rabbit tail scarfs, sling shots'.

'Foxer has a lot to lose which makes him dangerous, put these boxes on the boat, here you go. Forget about it.'

FrogFur pulls out one of the stonefish blades from his inside pocket and he hands the blade to Buxley. He cut the rope at the top so the sail dropped down with a huge pirate skull picture.

'I may be afraid of heights but danger is music I can dance too'

The next day was foggy with mild winds. The old Fox with one eye called 'one eyed mike' was ordering everyone to their starting positions. Even with one eye he noticed all teams were ready.

Frogfur put on his fog goggles to read his map and Buxley made his way towards the underground tunnels. The claxton rang aloud and each team swiftly started. FrogFur plucked the sail and paddles his way towards the fields.

Sound Of The Underground

Buxley took the lower tunnels swooping down through the leaves. He had a little glimpse at the other flying guardians, quickly dashing left into a tightly shut tunnel which led down. The tunnels were dark and damp. He flew as hard as he could to gain speed, each lantern he passed came flashing past like light glow sticks exploding at fireworks. Loud screams echoing behind him like chasing wolves. Ferrets lurking with nets ready to capture any guardian close enough in reach. If captured he was out of the race. Flapping past the large bookshelves, thousands of spider webs and dust swept in his eyes. He tried to keep a good flying distance in mid air, overlooking the ferret beds at the bottom. He was equipped with a silver crafted spare and his blade. Pacing through the tunnels he began to feel another flying guardian on his tail but couldn't grasp who it was. The sounds howling like ghosts at sea, it was scary and the smells changed like the seasons.

The ferrets in the burrows, jumping and ranting to catch any guardian in the dark. The glow sticks mapping a passage but still gazey when at speed. The furry winged animals flying past the underground maze was a spectacle. Buxley swerved into a small apartment rented by Mrs Goslin, an elderly ferret with her husband Makeroy an old veteran. She looked up at her ceiling as the crockery came crashing down.

Her first site of Buxley made her jump with fright, she swung her broom around crazily missing mostly. She threw down her cooking apron and Buxley spiralled up in a flying motion towards what looked like a window but it was barred closed.

Smash.

'Makeroyyyyyyyyyyyy!' she screams.

Her husband Makeroy runs in through the bathroom with his net, jumping off the wall he tries to swipe Buxley down to the ground. Buxley flew left madly swooping back through her kitchen, knocking pots and pans to the floor some more.

A loud cry from Mrs Goslin as Makeroy furiously jumps in the air trying to capture Buxley in his net. Buxley spun around sending Makeroy toppling over the sofa and speared his way through the old curtains into the passage, leaving a trail of cupcakes and plates on the floor. He somersaults through the door into another burrow house where he finds another ferret waiting. Jimmytoots. Jimmytoots spitfires two daggers that wisp pass Buxleys waistcoat, one piercing a slit in the pocket, his coat started to flap like propellers on a plane. Crumbs of honey biscuits start to fall out. Jimmytoots takes a slip and ends up head clean into a wall.

The guardian behind Buxley was Bramble, they fought blade to blade, tossing and turning through the tunnels. Barking from the last tunnel geared through his ears like a screeching car as Hugo came through with his spear separating the two. He was fast and dramatically flying, whisking his tail. Buxley threw his blade at the door handle which popped open as he kicked-pushed backwards through the tunnel. He called that move the backwards pig. He kept a keen eye as Hugo sped close near with Bramble bumping him side to side with his blade clenched against his spear. Buxley grabbed his flag and flew up out of the tunnels to the claxton.

It was down to FrogFur to make his round. Hoping for a good outcome Buxley and his backpack sat watching the screens at camp with the others that completed the dark underground tunnels.

Whilst Buxley sat at camp the fog had cleared and the night was warming. He sure was hungry. The catering prepared beans and caterpillar for lunch with worm sauce and crispy ant eggs. He ate and watched the screen as FrogFur and others made their way to the harbour of fields, a desolate place, stories of death and missing folks.

A spooky howl from the camp behind sent chills down his buxley's trotted legs. The fields were metres high stuck in inches of thick melted mud. In the mud were traps and in the traps were venom needles injected with toad tranquilliser.

Pre and her camera crew sat below in the trenches filming the teams entering. Large strikes of their machetes striking the grass. FrogFur has his wellingtons strapped with honey springs. This contraption would allow him to catapult out the mud if he stepped amongst the congestested traps.

He could hear the flying light bugs hovering over his head which gave him a sense of comfort. The fog now disappeared and dark whistles of a cold white moon approached. The machete cutting through.
Foxer snarling with his smoky cigar caught glimpse of his flag at distance. He checked his gold plated compass and held his binoculars to his smoky eyes.

He noticed that FrogFurs badge was a few metres closer so he began to machettey his way closer to FrogFur putting fox traps in the grass.

FrogFur lowered his flask into the water well. He filled up the flask when he caught FoxFur with the Gold Compass in the distance. He knew all he had to do was watch which direction Foxer went and he would find his Badge. However the Fox traps were now sinking into the mud and without his metal detector he would be surrounded. He made stilts with his machete and used his bonnoculers to pace towards what seemed like a badge. Uphill, downhill in between the willow trees and across mustard pond on oakland.

Suddenly he cut down a cage accidentally from the bushes bedded in thorns with his badge. It was a wild baby ferret cage with a note. It read 'carry me'. Inside was the golden compass and directions to camp.

Foxer was out of sight but cheers from camp drew near. The swamp like mud that was slugged on his boots squelched as he trod on. A dirty 18hrs later FrogFur turned up at camp exhausted holding the badge and the baby ferret clipped in its cage on his backpack with a handful of honeysuckle stems. FrogFur grabs buxley and smuggles him in his coat to pretend to suffocate him.

'Pigs can fly?'

'Yes, We certainly can……..was it lonely?' laughs Buxley sniffing at the cage.

'It was caged in the middle of the fields, here read the note' replied FrogFur

'It says carry me?'

'Yes'

'So you never asked where?'

'When it woke up the golden compass was in his little pillow. It was a cute moment.' replied FrogFur reaching for the snail gel and towel.

They made a small campfire and camped by the edge of the riverbank as FrogFur took a long shower to get rid of the mud in his ears and toes.

The next day FrogFur had lit the fire for breakfast and was lightly toasting cream dandelion leaves and bug burgers. They trained most of the day and played cards.

Later that night FrogFur was trying his best to read the map for the next event but was failing miserably. The speaker was calling teams for their next challenge. It was a cliff climb. The tallest hill in Mudhill Village.

They packed up the tent and opted for a green pond tea with fresh mint leaves. FrogFur powdered his hands with moth dust and began to put on his climbing equipment. Although Buxley could fly he had to hoist the cables connecting him and FrogFur like two twin bandits in a egg and spoon race. He also had to shine a torch so that they could see where to climb. The first team to the top would get a head start in the next challenge.
Buxley gave FrogFur a nudge as Foxer and Hugo approached with their boat across the other side of the bank, taunting words and throwing stones into the river.

'FrogFur you're still alive'

Foxer calls across in his husky voice, laughing with an evil grin. He was tall and thin and wore a military red coat, a white tailored shirt buttoned up to the neck showing his sleek defined body. He sneered, forking a pile of hay onto his boat.

'If you were a rodent and not a frog we could have been great friends, maybe even brothers?.'

'I agree."

FrogFur replies slowly, yawning with sarcasm.

'A frog scared of heights but lives in a tree, stupid comes to mind'

'A Fox piling hay and not in hiking equipment, ready to die included'

His red satin bag swung over his shoulder as a crowd of ferrets formed behind him. The squirrels began to mount in their canoes. FrogFur simply ignored him to unrope his boat as Buxley steered into the river heading to Willow Falls east of the cliff.

The celebrity squirrel Sid passed with his glam squad in tow, three assistants, and an organised entourage of rabbits screeching and wailing with excitement. He also was shooting a documentary about his life with CSN9.

Sid returned to Canada with his grandfather when he was six. So his accent was weirdly strange and he had his own style on the water. His long red locks groomed back into a thick ponytail. His face was carved to perfection with sparkling white teeth. He had a record of medals in snow sports. He was fond of keeping himself looking good. His boat almost collided with Pre as she and her reporters gathered on the water too.

'Good Morning and congratulations to all those who completed challenges yesterday. The fog is thickening but this competition is starting to get busy. Reports of stolen equipment and tampered boats have been the story of the day but If we can zoom in over those tree houses, you can see everyone looks fit to race and making their way. Undeniably the first day was somewhat frivolous. We have Bally Bramble here who was caught in the burrow race yesterday.

'...Hello Bally.'

'..Hello.'

'What can u tell us about yesterday?' she asks, pointing the microphone at his face.

'It's all a blur really, I did my best through the first few tunnels but when it got dark I couldn't see. I managed to duck a few ferrets but then got caught on the curve and was in the net. Couldn't believe it. The wife is embarrassed, the kids ain't talking to me.'

'So you were caught in the tunnels?'

'Yes.' he continues'

'Thank you Bally.'

FrogFur looked at his compass and map and knew they were a good few lunches away from the cliff. He thought about eating the last bug burger but thought to save it for the cliff, perhaps they had to sleep on a portaledge, a small hanging tent clipped on the edge of the cliff hanging mid air.

'Why do you let him wind you up?'

Who?'

'Foxer, who else?'

'Nothing like a revenge game to settle differences?'

'If that is spears you on, go for it'

FrogFur looks around and steers into the docks at The Hill. The toughest and roughest pond in PondLake. Every tree house was infested with gangs and notoriously known for having many food restaurants that sold alcohol.

A huge storm was approaching so for safety the cliff climb was cancelled. The bars and grills were full with teams and reporters. In the dock cabins the mice were supplying the wheat grain and conkers as treats for the supporters who camped outside. A make do situation.

Mice and Rice

Studley was by the darts with his nutmeg and oakbeer. His arms were covered in tattoos which drew from his shoulders down to his wrist. His giant ears were pierced with rubies and diamonds, a gift from his four fathers as a child.

He lived in Mudhill Village and had 4,000 children and 7,000 great grandchildren and an uncounted number of brothers and sisters. He cleaned his teeth with a sharp dart whilst standing in Slug Pot the seafood restaurant.

He dragged his crown round and fixed his waistcoat, his gold shining badge honoured by Princess Chip for his military involvement in the war shining bright in the evening darkness. He particularly loved to tell stories and was a very wise mouse indeed. One last sip of his oakbeer, placing his thin pink lips around his goblet. His silk grey fur slickly lay wet on his face like a drowning rat. A giant thunder sound echoed through the restaurant rattling the windows. The restaurant went quiet.

FrogFur and the others including Sid and Foxer were approaching the port in their boats. Each paddling heavy in the spiteful storm behind them. Foxer was paddling hard and thick. His face was drenched and he had his blade tightly clenched between his teeth.

Barbican, despite being warned not to, had made his way to warn the others of the storm. Suddenly a huge lightning struck, the bridge came tumbling down. The loud crash was like an explosion, fireworks of rock and stone flew up into the air, trees pelting down like hail stones. Over flooding the port, boats capsizing and mice being plunged into the water drowning as the winds wisped in waves.

The others looked on in horror. There was silence. The bridge continued to fall. An alarm was signalled and the swim guards jumped in to save who they could. Foxer was searching for Hugo screaming at the top of his lungs. Buxley took several dives into the water to search for FrogFur as their boat split into two like a pizza slice.

'FrogFur!'

Buxley was dragged away by a swim guard. The storm hailing. Boats crashing into homes and children screaming. It was an armageddon of water and wind. News travelled back to the pond and tears were shared amongst all. The rain continued to fall and the lightning horrendously barricaded every river and barge. The rivers were flooded. The storm forced everyone high above ground in the village top trees.

A few hours later in Slug Pot. The place was hurdled with benches and tables brought in by the swim guards. Soaking wet towels laid everywhere. The owner had roped his entire restaurant up in the trees with ropes and cables. Barely keeping still like a rocking horse.

Buxley smothered in mud sat glued to the telly watching Princess Chip's report from the palace. Bugger was fixing the aerial with his small yellow raincoat on top of the roof looking down at the rivers merged into one.

Alber, uncertain of FrogFur, started to cry. She remembered the boat being smashed by the bridge and lost sight of what happened next. Buxley flew over to comfort her.

The whole entire pond was in a state of emergency. The village river houses were destroyed, boats, families were missing children. The swim guards did their best to patrol the area and hours later gave up on the search for any survivors.

Morning rose. The sun started to peak up like nosey kids at a barbeque. Studley was running as fast as he could. His ears were falling back at the speed he was racing to get to the palace. Chestnut City the city built on acres of cobbled paths, vine yards and carriages courting gold. He slid under the vineyard gate and continued to run right into a side alley towards the entrance of the palace. Two grasshoppers stood both surprised at the little mouse which stood beneath them panting for breath.

'Sir Studley'

The larger grasshopper bends down.

'Come back tomorrow, No visitors today'

He tossed Studley to the wall sending him smashing to the ground, his silky grey hair went spiky and his sharp claws piercing from his hands began to spawn.

'This is a matter of urgency, I must come through!' he demands.

'Can't you hear. No Entry!'

He shoves Studley again. Studley's eyes turn red as he jumps up and slashes the grasshopper twice in the face. He kicks and claws the other grasshopper's legs, sending them both crying to the ground with pain. He cuts past the gates as his tail whips them both in the eyes leaving them momentarily blind.

He ran through the gates which lead through a path of these wonderful chambers with gold bathrooms and high ceilings. The halls were traditionally decorated with marble floors. He slid around the corner alerting four more grasshopping guards who began to chase him. He climbed up through the chapel tower and swung down the bell into the garden. Speeding through the meadows suddenly he saw a great large trail appear from behind the tree.

'Princess.....'

Her eyes appeared from behind the fountain. Her grey gown covered in rhinestones and crystals with her umbrella resting to her side.

'The village is in danger. We have no more room.You must lower the capital bridge.'

'I will not. No more boats can come in or out.'

She replies waving the guards to stop running.

'Princess. This storm has destroyed everything.'

'I have spoken with Foxer. He has assured me he has this under control. I suggest you trust him and wait for further instructions.'

'Foxer will say whatever to keep the treasury. He cannot be trusted. He does not care the village'

'So what is your request?

Princess you must lower the bridge, there are children, thousands.' he replies.

'The children shall find haven in the treehouse by monument, That is all I can do now. You should be looking for FrogFur. I hear he also has not been found? seen as you have several hours to spare?

'My importance is to make sure the water doesn't collapse the entire village?'

'Studley. I've known you a very long time and have always admired your integrity and wise stories you so fondly tell in that pub that sells beer and worms. All those who return for the final race will be listed for the treasury. Time is in your favour' she smiles

'Thank you Princess Chip.'

Vacation

FrogFur had made quarters in a billion year old oak tree. Roots touching the hells of earth. Once the bridge came crumbling down on top of him he hit into a drain which flushed him out into an abandoned reservoir.
He hunted and found an old crate of canned mushrooms, an old record player with a broken radio aerial and a handmade fishing net. The berries on the tree were starting to run out and his stomach was making grouchy sounds. He was hungry. The radio was on, updating him of the weather but how far he was to the village he still did not know.

He made shelter in the tree for weeks. Casually nodding off to the sound of the radio and humming insects in the distance. His beard is now grown. His clothes looked two sizes too small and he was missing everyone. However the radio warned the bridge had damaged the rivers making it impossible to get to Pond Lake especially without a boat.

The morning after the rain had finally stopped. He could finally see the sky. He climbed down the tree using his rope stabbing his blade in the tree for harnessing. As he hit the water a huge rusty looking barge appeared out of nowhere.

'Oi Watch Out'

'Oh rats mud. what have I done?' says a light voice from the top of the barge. It was Sir Tod, Princess Spec and Phoebe. Sir Tod switches off the engine to have a closer look.

'Oh dear'.

'Is he dead?'

Spec sat on the edge of the barge sticking a stick up his nose and poking his belly.

'Yes I think you killed him.' said Phoebe wondering how Spec had just killed an innocent frog in the middle of a derelict reservoir.

He laid in the water as they dragged him out onto the barge. Spec with her freckles leaned in close to his face, noticing something strange.

'Grandfather, He looks familiar. I think he's the missing frog on the news. The frog on the posters. We should hand him in. Ten thousand crowns for him grandfather. We can say he was dead when we found him.'

'Spec behave, cruel is never cute.'

'Ten thousand is a lot of crowns' said Phoebe

FrogFur started to wake slowly unnoticed. Sir Tod roped his barge around the tree securing it tightly.

'Girls wait here. Leave his pockets alone Phoebe. Spec release the anchor at the back. I'm going to see what is up in this tree. I can hear a radio.'

'Daisy cakes?'.

Spec yells. Sid cricketty legs scramble up the tree. Her butterflies lifting her long metal dress across the deck of the barge to lower the anchor.

'Maybe'.
Sir Tod drops a bag down into the water and Phoebe hooks them onto the boat.

'Mushrooms.' she says in disgust.

'Salted Mushrooms.'

'Like what the slugs bum do you think you worm skins are doing? Those mushrooms are mine.'

Sir Tod jumps from the nearest branch onto the barge and stands face to face with FrogFur. Both fish blades are drawn. Spec cohearsing Tod to fish him like a gutted trout. However what happened next was extremely unlikely.

'I don't want to have to hurt you, just get off my barge and be on our way.'

'Give me the radio and the bag the little one is hiding.'

'Little.' whispers Spec totally insulted.

Sir Tods hands over the other bag and they leave. The next day the smell of scented daisy buttercup cakes, rose soup and chestnut coffee was in the morning air.

FrogFur couldn't help but swim across the reservoir to the smell. Delicious daisy butter cups. Light, fluffy and nutritious.

'Oh look Grandfather. It's him.'

'Play nice Spec. The smell of daisy cakes can make anyone learn to swim'

'Would you care to join us?'

'I'd be delighted too'

Spec continued icing the cakes with Phoebe in the kitchen. FrogFur climbed aboard hangin his feet off the side of the boat in wonder.

They spoke for hours, eating and sharing stories. Sir Tod gave a master class of hidden maps and rivers. Which is how they were able to find the reservoir with a billion year old oak tree even though the gates were locked.

'There are many hidden places in the Pond. If your as inquisitive as spec you'd find them'

They looked at the map and began to sail back towards the Pond. Studley revved his water bike across the reservoir. It was small enough to fit through the gates and his consent to search for missing villagers from Princess Chip helped the guards allow him through. As the barge sail hit the wind slowly easing the barge out to the river linked to the reservoir.

Studley started to see empty salted mushroom cans floating. Rose soup smelling in the air, a distinctive smell. He was close to something, not sure what.

'The billion year old tree? I thought that was a myth.'

He mutters to himself as he approaches the barge. FrogFur was on the front deck washing his feet.

'Salted Slugging Mushrooms!'

'Studley!'

'FrogFur, It is you. We thought you were dead, you must come with me now.'

'Slow down Studley. I'm on vacation. Have a cake. It's dandelion with berries.'

'This is serious. We must tell Foxer. Him and his bandit gang have taken over. There is no electricity. My children are scared to go out at night. There has been break ins and fires. It is villainous.'

'The bridge collapsed and drained me right out across the river. I had no idea.' He takes the map and shows Studley how quick to get back to the pond. They both put on their life jackets and board the water bike.

Sir Tod, using his new fish blade to fondle with some equipment gives a subtle nod at Spec who swooshes over with Phoebe tagging not far behind.

'I was going to hand you in but Grandfather said no. I trusted him. Do you trust this mice with the funny teeth?
If Foxer knows you're alive he will start preparing for the final boat race. As you have no boat I don't think that is the smartest thing to do. If you win you'll be able to help us all. Why don't we build you a boat here? I have more dandelion cakes and caterpillar garlic bread? '

Her sweet innocent voice was hard to ignore. FrogFur slouches over the barge chewing a stick of wheat. His time with Sir Tod had taught him a great deal. Family was important and Buxley was in the village with that filthy Foxer and his unwanted rejects.

'I am many things, but a coward is not one. Studley lead the way'.

Spec turned the engine on and captained the boat towards Village following instruction from Sir Tod. She gave ForgFur a paper bag full of daisy cakes and Pheobe got a signed wanted poster which she stuck on her sleeping bag with honey.

Buxley snuck FrogFur through the burrow tunnels and they camped far from the others. The village was exactly how Studley described chaos, bandit boulevard.
FrogFur wore a ski mask covering his face to shop for tools to build the boat. His beard still grown. His herb diet of sparkling hill fresh water to increase his agility and swimming strength. He practised repetitively, diving, climbing, deep dips improving his strategy to be light on the water and ride the waves.

Spec made arrangements with Bamear to design a new wetsuit for his race secretly. The wetsuit was handmade and tailored without any measurements. The debutant collaboration between Stones and Islands, Cortex, Global and partners created something special, visionaries of pond fashion.

May 8 2014

Bamear lived in a luxury apartment in chestnut city, sharing his tree lodge with Stone. He had a unique sense of style. He had started his own business when he was four when he designed the dress Princess Fiona wore on her birthday. His round hut boutique shop in a river gated garden was fabulous. Handmade dresses and jewellery. Appointment only fittings.

He sat at his desk when a small bug ran in through the pig flap, he turned towards the bug who looked out of breath. The big hands Bamear a small tin of gold coins.

Days to the race the sun had returned beating heat hardening the soil. Most of the rivers firmly fenced in by the swim guards and palace patrons. Rebecca and Fiona had returned to the palace from Highland with King Roy Jnr.

FrogFur was out jogging across the grass as the horns from the city palace echoed down through the hills. The announcement of the final water race. The high swings and ropes made during the flood ribboned down into the water, ripples of tangled vines and battered bramble bushes and crushed lily pads. The pond had never looked so devastatingly beautiful.

Fury In The Forest

A collaboration of wooden arrows, maps and tools were packed. Studley sharpen the blades with his teeth. It was starting to get hysterical.
Hugo with a fairly crafted boat of planks pulled into the river as he spots a shaved FrogFur standing still with a glare of redemption.

'I guess the guards enjoyed playing hide and seek with you during the storm. You think you can win?'

FrogFur grabs his fish blade sussing out the trailing boat behind.

'Can you sound anymore crazy? I have found my way here just like you.'

'You ran away.' replies Hugo.

'I got rid of the dead weight.'

'Foxer will have you eating his leftovers once he wins and is given the treasury again' he laughs.

FrogFur slowly loads his slingshot with his mud stones. As starts pelting Hugo into the river.

'Help.'

Hugo climbed on to his boat covered in stone conkers attracting thousands of water ants from below the water. The water ants eventually covered the entire boat. His face was covered in ant bites.

'Hugo you flying rodent. Carry my message to Foxer. Game on .'

Hugo was taken away for treatment and the boat was almost unusable. Once he arrived at the starting bay he looked around at trees broken in the river like traffic islands. FrogFur jumped out and threw his rucksack over his shoulder. The tree huts were pretty low to the ground with smartly cut hedges and semi-detached gardens, the shiny glass house at the gates was stocked with crates and large containers of sparkling spring water.

Foxer's cousins were howling at chippie the swimguard about cargo regulations. They initially ordered four crates per boat. Foxer had sixteen which was not allowed. The neighbouring restaurant managers came to the gate to get their delivery and were annoyed at the waiting time so they started to protest. A search was warranted.

Chippie the swimguard dived down into the water to have a closer look at the bottom of the boats. He noticed the cargo strapped on the bottom of the boat contained a fortress of traps and rural weapons.

The tag read 'Hugo, 298 Park River'. When Hugo finally arrived on a stretcher, he was arrested whilst taken to hospital. A cute exit for such a fiery cheat.

A few bushfires away it was a carnival atmosphere brewing . Foxer had torn every poster down from every tree in the forest and was trashing all the gardens that were not supporting him.

The night sky had covered the pond. The moon being the only light painted across the water. The only bar opened was Slug Pot. They cooked seaweed slugs roasted in garlic and cheese, grilled potato pie topped with black spiders and unsalted mushrooms. The slug juice smoothie was a favourite with a hint of ant pepper and minted worms.

The Slug Pot had been open for years. It was nostalgic and had computer games and an open pool fish tank. It was like a spaceship inside with swinging candelabras in the main seating area. They sold expensive bottles of mustard and lemon sauce. The concierge housed some of the most expensive boats tech blast inc had built. It was the only restaurant that was waterproof and fireproof and had insurance. This was because of the veteran customers.

Many rated the food the best. Well some say Bug Kebabs and the owner of Slug Pot were cousins. The grandparents of a water buffalo and a bear. Who knows?

The orders were in. Foxer and Sid sat at the table. The waitress tabled their apple crush drinks on napkins and left her number for Sid on the side plate. Foxer took a swig of his drink, twisting his whiskers. A live news coverage showing FrogFur arriving at the canal park was repeated on the sports channel.

'Something needs to be done.' he grunts.

'I will lay my neck on the sharpest slaughter block before I allow this peasant of a crown to win'. he continues

The apple crushed drinks melting by the warm heat in his breath as he spoke. The waiter carries the trays of hot seafood platters.

'Sea worms, soup, garlic chips?'

Foxer points at Sid and his cousins. Their plates flung down like hot baking trays in a bakers.

'Do we still have a chance? Without the traps?

'Pipe down Sid. That was Hugo's boat, not ours, remember?.'

'Yes.'

Foxer grabs his scarf and sneaks through a backdoor leaving Sid the bill. A few hours passed and FrogFur had found somewhere to stay. An old ladybug offered him a room. He lit his lamp and read the map of the lakes and rivers with his magnifying glass. He insisted on using everything he had learned for the race but his stomach was growling.

He takes a canal cab to Slug Pot but when he arrives he realised his ski mask is not in his fur coat. With it already being late and ladybug looking ever so tired he decides to go in anyway. The chef walks over with a smoking grill, mushrooms stuffed with garlic, a bottle of red berry juice in an ice bucket.

'We smoke our mushrooms with ant egg peppers, garlic, and grill gently with our famous vegan seafood sauce. The drinks come with main. Here is our menu. We are fully booked but we are doing takeaway tonight?'

FrogFur covering and shielding ladybug as they scurry through the tables and chairs to the front of house desk.

'You' he says, startled.

'Follow me. It is not safe here'

He takes them to the fish pool as quickly as a butterfly jump. The waiter passed the news to the kitchen and Nazy the manager made all waitresses aware when Foxer came in to make sure he didn't go to the fish pool.

'We have a very special guest tonight, let's cook him a winning meal.'

They delivered fourteen piping hot plates meanwhile a suspicious Sid was searching the premises with Able the guard who was questioning. He wanted to know how the fox traps got into Hugo's boat. He also wanted to talk with Foxer, who was avoiding all security.

Able took a table outside to have something to eat, exhausted from all the detective work. Sid also cunningly sat close asking questions of his own.

'So you have no idea how those traps got there? Hugo has said nothing? This is scary. I have not travelled across the Pond to be hurt in an accident that could have been prevented. If you hear anything let my agent know. I have insurance'

Any connection to him and crime would destroy his image. The play bunnies would move onto Hakim in Highland and he would literally be casted as a bandit.

Inside Fletcher the bullfighter from Columbia was making the last few cocktails for FrogFur and Ladybug. They were now full and stomach warm with delicious dandelion cakes and chocolate mud custard.
The cocktails were crushed ice, ginger, peppered squids with lemon. FrogFur bagged his leftovers, jerk fungi and a few cakes for ladybug.

Fletcher kindly offered to take them back home as the ladybug fell asleep at the table, her reading glasses hanging on the end of her sweet button cupped nose, snoring quietly.

The next morning was race day. FrogFur was brushing his teeth outside by the water tap when he noticed something very unusual about the shed door lock. He potted his toothbrush in the cup and walked slowly towards the shed. The lock had been broken during the night but his racing raft was still there. The shed door creaked back open and standing there were two strong faced foxes, towering over him like a dying willow tree.

'500,000 gold crowns to take you back to the city chambers for questioning.'

'Let me go. I have something for Foxer. Here. It will help him win'

The foxes offer their attention.

'It's a map of the winning route and sapphire gemstone with gold encrusted stones. It IS worth more than five hundred thousand crowns. You have to trust me, This is what Foxer wants.'

They take the map and walk out slowly crunching the fist together.

'If this is a stitch up. We will come back and visit ladybug too.'

FrogFur travelled to the start of the race towing his raft through the village with supporters following behind cheering. When he arrived he witnessed a spectacular view of the pond he'd never had seen before.

'White! Franco! What the pigs fart is going on?

Franco dried himself off with a towel and walked over to FrogFur embracing a solid hug. White dived in from the top tree splashing the supporters as he grabbed FrogFur but the legs lifting him up in the air.

'Can u believe it?. A thousand moons and yet here he stands. Alive.'

'We thought you were dead. We were coming to seek revenge for Uncle Arthur and Tonyius. Tear whoever to threads like cloth. Cut the tails and bury the bones'.

White smiles, showboating his bow and arrow to the crowd. FrogFur was so fond of his cousins. He pulled his boat into the water hoisting his pirate flag high in the air.

'Im fine. How did you get here?'.

'We took a plane? You still remember what a plane is?'

'Yes'

White had joined the army and been away for years. His mum was FrogFurs Aunty. He always kept in contact and sent canned goods anytime he was on duty close to Pond Lake. His big Brother Franco was living in the Alps of Highland as a golf instructor. They both grew up with FrogFur and really teased him being an only child. They came to see the race and were cheerleading as he stood at the starting line.

The supporters took to their seats and the news crews were hovering in air balloons. The starter checks were under way. The boats were checked and security made sure there wasn't any hydraulics in the engines, traps, unlisted weapons or damaged equipment.

A million rivers and dusty moons hailing in the distance and the sun slowly tiptoed through the clouds. The pink sunset kissed the top of the starter pistol.

FrogFur zipped up his wetsuit and tied his jellies to his webbed feet. He shoved his bag of conkers in his rucksack before adjusting his sail.
Foxer shoved his blade into his pocket. His stern sharp teeth grizzled in tight between his lips.

'You're going to challenge me, You dare?' he snarls.

A loud cheer from the crowd. FrogFur looked straight ahead down the river. Holding his engine gauge ready to splurge into position.

'Clear the water' a swimguard shouts.

The fishing boat engineers scrambled out the shallow waters leaving only the racers. FrogFur put on his water goggles. Sid a few boats down the line, tied his long lobster red hair up in a bun giving FrogFur a long glare as Foxer paddled up beside him. They were in cahoots but it didn't matter. The race was about to start.

A great last look on to the horizon before the pistol halted a loud bang into the air. The race has started. The crowd cheered and the FrogFur took position like he planned. His engine held a good speed to get into 1st position. Sid sliding close 2nd.

Sid somersaults over FrogFur, his ponytail whipping past his face in slow motion, perfectly landing on his boat. The crowd goes wild. Another Frog plummets forward but crashes into the banks as the sharp turn to the left is barricaded by a fallen tree.

Frogfur swiftly scoops under the bridge, long strokes in the water keeping a steady pace. His sail catches the wind as they approach yet another turn. Suddenly from behind Foxer drew his paddle to FrogFur's neck as his boat went up close.

FrogFur strikes back. Foxer hits again. FrogFur strikes back again. He reaches for his bow and arrow, ties rope to the bow and shoots a tree. He used the rope to steer left around the wave and down into 1st position again.

Foxers eyes were lit with fire. The water cascading through their legs and drowning their feet. The anticipation of the next few moves was dangerous. Sid paddling furiously to keep up. Foxer drew his blade again to cut yet another sail to get more speed.

The river crept round the last willow tree. FrogFur could see the finishing line. He paddle faster and harder and sat in the driving seat steering over the waterfall and down into the last turn to the finishing line.

Foxer drew for the map which had the secret route. He leaned his boat to the left which ran through stinging nettles and rose thorns. The map was a fake. The real map was hidden. Even today nobody knows where.

FrogFur laid chest down as he came to turn by the willow tree. The speed going over 100 mph. Sid had no chance of catching up and Foxer was still struggling with the rose thorns screaming at security.

FrogFur knotted his sail to his back like a parachute. He passes the finishing line, slowing down just in time. No casualties.

The parachute idea was new. The speed was never going to stop him but saving his raft from destruction was a skill he learned.
He swam over to Studley, Chip and Alber who hugged him and cheered even louder. Buxley who had been at home on security orders flew around their home screaming to the neighbours FrogFur had won.

The crowd chanted his name. Sir Tod and Spec were dancing with joy. The crowns and champion ribbon attached to his raft as news reporters took pictures recording live with a sense of passion and drive for such a fast engineered race.

Studley was crying in Slug Pot as he sipped his oak beer by the dart board. He was awfully proud. He had kept his promise to support all from the Pond as his veteran allegiance had taught him.

The treasury was signed and handed to FrogFur. The acres of land with the honeysuckle bushes, the gold crowns, wishing worms and a garage close to home for any other races he may want to compete thus the new days ahead.

9 781716 050275